LISBON CONFIDENTIAL

HIDDEN GEMS LOVED BY LOCALS

AUTHORS: FANY PÉCHIODAT, LAURIANE GEPNER AND LUCIE ETCHEBERS
ILLUSTRATIONS: COLINE GIRARD
PHOTOS: PAULA FRANCO @LISBONBYLIGHT

JONGLEZ PUBLISHING
Travel guides

ATUM NATURAL
MINOR

‘FOR A LONG TIME,
WE KEPT THIS CODE WORD
TO OURSELVES: LISBON.

IF THINGS TOOK A BAD TURN,
THE WHITE CITY WOULD BE
OUR SAFE HAVEN.’

OLIVIER FRÉBOURG

WHAT YOU WON'T FIND
IN THIS GUIDE

- the route of Tram 28
- the address of the Santa Justa elevator
- the most touristy dinner and fado show

WHAT YOU WILL FIND
IN THIS GUIDE

- bars that only locals go to
- the joy of running on clouds
- a party venue the size of a palace
- fifty shades of green in the middle of the city
- the best spots of Marvilla

This guide is not comprehensive – and it doesn't aspire to be. There are other guides for that.
Our M.O. is the opposite of overwhelming you with options. Instead of suggesting 1,000 ideas you won't have time to explore in just a few days anyway, we've chosen around 30. Obviously, we were very tempted to stretch that to 40, or even 50 ... But we stuck to our guideline. As a result, we scoured Lisbon without counting our steps, climbed and hurtled back down hills, chatted with the characters who crossed our path, sampled every edible thing to be found in the city, drank a few nectars (guided by our professional code of ethics) and explored all the nooks and crannies, passages and alleyways ...

And here you are, holding the fruits of our labour in your hands. A selection of experiences in Lisbon to savour, make your own and we hope – love.

SYMBOLS USED IN
LISBON CONFIDENTIAL

< 10 euros

10 to 40 euros

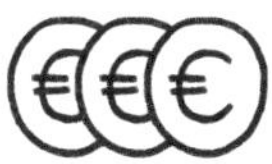

> 40 euros

First come,
first served

Reservation
recommended

100% Lisbon

Opening times often vary,
so we recommend checking them directly
on the website of the place you plan to visit.

Some call it magnetic; others compare it to an aging woman who has lost almost all her finery but still has style. Some claim it's eternal; others that it's losing its soul as the face of the city changes. Maybe the truth can be found – as is so often the case – at the intersection of history, memories and dreams, both collective and personal. Somewhere in a tram lurching across the ages and hills; in the dusky pink of a façade in Mouraria, blushing as a ray of sunlight skims it just so; in the beating heart of the city, Chiado; in the cheeky humour of Graça; or in the majesty of Belém. In the *miradouros* perched on the city's highest points. And, finally, in the Tagus River, which flows into the ocean across which the great 15th- and 16th-century Portuguese explorers set sail and returned home.

Lisbon is like the movement of these waves, flowing between the open ocean and shore. Are we in a can't-miss capital of the start-up scene, a young and creative city, forward-looking and tech-driven? Or in one of Europe's oldest cities, covered with azulejo tiles, whose thousands of blue eyes have been watching us, unblinking, for several centuries? The answer is: both. Lisbon juggles with time, jumping from past to near future across two thresholds. Here, a supremely Instagrammable coffee shop with clean lines; there, a boutique that's been around since 1789 and still makes candles the old-fashioned way – today as it did yesterday, as it will tomorrow. Or maybe not: Lisbon's fate is cause for concern. The old boutiques are closing their doors; with each façade that is renovated, a bit more of the Lisbon of yesterday disappears.

Yet there's one thing about Lisbon that isn't ready to change: the light. So unique it could give anyone the crazy idea never to leave the city again – or to leave everything else for it. A light born of the reflection of the water on the Tagus, called the 'Sea of Straw' (Mar da Palha) for its golden shimmer. A light that paints the cobblestones white, splashing across everything in its way, the façades dancing along with it like shadow puppets. Lisbon is written in this eternal light, of which one Lisbon native said, 'I've never seen similar light anywhere else. Grey days are my favourite: the cobblestones are of such pure white they seem to be infinite in volume.' She then went on: 'Lisbon is a poem to look at.' We'd add: 'and to discover.'

ANTONIO
KNIFE-SHARPENER

01. Some of the hotels we really like
02. The temple of Portuguese cuisine
03. Sink your teeth into a *bifana*
04. See a film under the open skies
05. Three bar stools, one bar
06. Rooms with views: Lisbon at your feet
07. Running laps on a rooftop
08. Go for a stroll in the Estufa Fria
09. An American diner, Lusitanian style
10. Lisbon's best concept store
11. Dive into Lisbon's secret underground
12. An aperitif under the stars on Lisbon steps
13. Small cafe, wide angle
14. Uncover the secret spot where fado singers hide away
15. A fantastic bar that has resisted Alfama's gentrification
16. Colourful cuisine
17. Music, cocktails and tapas
18. A unique tea emporium
19. Bar, bookstore, cinema, concerts, DJ sets ... An essentiel venue
20. A historic venue, far from the in-crowds of tourists
21. Soak up the atmosphere of Praça das Flores
22. Just our kind of bar
23. A bar off the beaten track
24. *Pastéis de nata* vs elephant ears: showdown of the sweets
25. A bistro just the way we like it
26. A masterpiece of a Japanese restaurant
27. Grilled fish at Ponto Final
28. Experience a surreal evening
29. A Berlin club in Lisbon
30. Discovering the east of the city
31. An alternative night out in Marvila

9
8
28 29
30 31
7
23
4
10
6
11
1
1
24
1
12
21
20
13
25
22
19
5
BAIRRO ALTO
15
14
4
3
16
BAIXA CHIADO
2
6
Alfama
3
17 18
1
26
nte
DE ABRIL
27
Almada

#01

SOME OF THE HOTELS **WE REALLY LIKE**

Lisbon is full of charming hotels but of course not all are worth stopping by. Here's our pick.

> **Palácio Príncipe Real**

Housed in a palace built in 1877, Palácio Príncipe Real hotel is perfectly sited, as its name suggests, just a few steps from Príncipe Real and a minute's walk from the charming Praça das Flores (see p. 93).

Lovely azulejos in one of the lounges, large bedrooms, a magnificent swimming pool and an internal garden (rare in central Lisbon), a perfect welcome from English owners Miles and Gail ... All in all, a quality location.

€€€

PALÁCIO PRÍNCIPE REAL
R. DE SÃO MARÇAL 77

palacioprincipereal.com | Instagram: @palacioprincipereal

© PALÁCIO PRÍNCIPE REAL

© FRANCISCO NOGUEIRA

PHOTOS © YVES DURONSOY

> Tarabel Lisbon

In the charming residential district of Lapa, but just minutes from some of the best restaurants in Lisbon, the Tarabel is one of the most beautiful hotels in the city (maybe even the most beautiful?), just like its big brother in Marrakesh. Wildly refined decoration, a charming welcome, a great swimming pool at the end of the terraced garden and quality cuisine reserved for guests ... A tremendous success.

€€€

TARABEL LISBON
R. SACRAMENTO À LAPA 15

+351 21 405 0450	tarabellisbon.com	Instagram: @tarabellisbon

> **Santa Clara 1728**

There are places that exist beyond the limits of time, trends and words. The Santa Clara 1728 hotel is one of them. Within the walls of this 18th-century palace, six rooms and a table d'hôte straight out of a minimalist dream are a blend of white, beige, blond wood and authentic period stone. Outside, in the world at large, our attention is constantly being solicited. Here, behind the Santa Clara's large doors and its windows overlooking the National Pantheon, in these rooms in which nothing is superfluous, silence reigns, the mind grows calm and sets sail, the soul takes flight ...

Which is one definition of luxury.

€€€

SANTA CLARA 1728
CAMPO DE SANTA CLARA 128, RC

+351 93 225 1056

silentliving.pt/houses/santa-clara-1728

SANTA CLARA 1728
© PIERRE VERDOUX

> **Montecarmo 12**

Designed by the same architectural firm (Atelier Aires Mateus) as Santa Clara 1728 but with a more reasonable budget, Montecarmo 12 is an excellent address.

The pretty rooms, each equipped with an elegant, understated stone bathtub, are arranged around the beautiful spiral staircase that encapsulates the soul of this revamped historic residence in the heart of the Principe Real district.

They serve a delicious breakfast too.

€€€

HOTEL MONTECARMO 12
TV. MONTE DO CARMO 12

+351 21 096 3549 | montecarmo12.com | Instagram: @montecarmo12

© NELSON GARRIDO

- JOÃO RODRIGUES -

MANAGER OF THE SILENT LIVING GUESTHOUSES

João Rodrigues juggles gracefully. In addition to his career as an airline pilot, he also owns four exceptional guesthouses in Portugal, including Santa Clara 1728 in Lisbon. We met him over a classic breakfast.

What made you want to open guesthouses?
When I was little, my parents' home was always open and filled with people. That inspired me for the future!

What's the story behind Santa Clara 1728?
The first time I saw this building, it was under renovation. I climbed the façade and that's when I fell for the view: the National Pantheon on one side, the convent and monastery of São Vicente de Fora on the other, and, in the far background, the Tagus. I knew I had to live here and open a guesthouse in this old neighborhood tucked between Alfama and Graça.

How would you define the 'Silent Living' philosophy?
It permeates Santa Clara, whose

© PHILIPPA LANGELY

INTERVIEW

large volumes recall an ancient monastery. It's about respecting traditional architecture and materials, developing a minimalist esthetic around them, and distilling an atmosphere that's reminiscent of a family home ... And, at the heart of this philosophy is the idea that when you enter here, you leave behind the hustle and bustle and demands of the outside world – everything that disturbs peace of mind.

What's your view of Lisbon?
The Tagus embraces the city, opening its arms wide to it. That's what moves me most about this city: its connection to the water. And for me, as someone who is always on the move as part of my profession, Lisbon is the home that welcomes me with open arms every time I return.

Your favorite places?
The Gulbenkian Museum, its gardens, which are the work of Portugal's best landscape designers. I also love Belém, even though it has changed over the years. When I try to go back to a place, I'd like to reconnect with my memories; often it isn't possible because it has closed down or been replaced ...

© NELSON GARRIDO

Is that what's meant by *saudade*?
Yes. It has to do with our history, the age of great discoveries in the 15th and 16th centuries. People left, and you never knew if they would return. That's the origin of this feeling of absence, this nostalgia – a powerful emotion.

One last Lisbon secret?
The best time to enjoy the city is ... in February. The streets are emptier, time is distilled more slowly, and the light is as gorgeous as ever.

PRADO
TRAVESSA DAS PEDRAS NEGRAS 2

+351 21 053 4649

pradorestaurante.com
Instagram: @prado_restaurante

#02

THE TEMPLE OF **PORTUGUESE NOUVELLE CUISINE**

Prado means 'meadow' in Portuguese. And that's where chef Antonio Galapito, aka the rising star of Portugal's food scene, takes his inspiration. After having learned the ropes with chef Nuno Mendes in London, Galapito now champions 'cuisine libre' (free cuisine) at his Lisbon restaurant, inspired by the farm-to-table movement. Ingredients that come from all across the country, dishes whose composition changes daily depending on the season and the chef's mood ... The only constant: the flavour of Portugal today.

- ANTONIO GALAPITO -

CHEF AT PRADO

What's your oldest cooking-related memory?
I was born near Sintra, where suckling pig is a specialty. Maybe even more than the taste, it's the smell of it that makes my mouth water ... My mother would grill it over a wood fire, and you could smell the aroma of garlic, paprika, white wine, and black pepper.

Do you serve it at Prado?
Sometimes, but cooking it for seven to eight hours in a normal oven is a bit more technical. The way we serve it is also different from the traditional recipe: meat, sauce, and ... that's it. Bye-bye, trimmings. The meat is so tender, there's no need for anything else.

When did you know you wanted to become a chef?
When I was 14, I was terrible at school. I wasn't passionate about cooking; I didn't even particularly love eating – in fact, for me, a good steak was a well-done steak, which gives you some idea ... But that's when my mother suggested I go to cooking school. So I went – and never looked back.

And if you were to do something else ...?
No, I don't see myself doing anything else. Or maybe a farmer, when I'm 60 years old?

Is Prado a Portuguese restaurant?

Yes, to the extent that we source all of our ingredients (except for sugar) from Portuguese food producers all across the country. That's our only rule, and we build our menu – which changes a bit every day, depending on what gets delivered and our inclinations – around it. When we see new fish, we always ask if it was caught in Portuguese waters. If not, we don't take it!

Your à-la-carte guilty pleasure?

It varies every day, but some dishes are always on the menu and don't change much. One of my favorites (maybe even my absolute favorite!) is the bread, served with a paste made of goat's-milk butter, smoked coarse salt, pork fat, garlic, and caramelised onion compote ... I can't get enough of it!

A fun fact about Portuguese cuisine?

The Portuguese have always been great travelers. Did you know that they brought tempura to Japan? And when they returned from their expeditions, they brought back yuzu, which now grows in Portugal. We use it in the Prado kitchens instead of lemon: it immediately transports you to another place.

PHOTOS © RODRIGO CARDOSO

#03

SINK YOUR TEETH **INTO A *BIFANA***

A *bifana* is to the Portuguese what a ham-and-cheese sandwich is to the British: a simple, quick and inexpensive solution that rarely disappoints. It consists of a very finely sliced pork cutlet, marinated in dry white wine, lemon juice, bay leaves, paprika and garlic, and gently basted in its own juices, nestling between two slices of *papo seco* (Portuguese bread). To spice things up, spread on some mustard right before you sink your teeth into it and then wash it down with a few glasses of wine. For an even more decadent experience, bite into a *leitão*, a typical Portuguese sandwich made with suckling pig.

For *bifanas*:	For *leitãos*:
AS BIFANAS DO AFONSO **R. DA MADALENA 146**	**NOVA POMBALINA** **RUA DO COMÉRCIO 2**
instagram.com/explore/locations/440586039731769/as-bifanas-do-afonso	+351 21 887 4360

OVA POMBALINA

CINE SOCIETY

#04

SEE A FILM UNDER THE OPEN SKIES

Around when the sun sets over the Tagus, one of the great pleasures Lisbon has to offer is watching a film in an open-air cinema.

> **Cine Society**

Perched on the rooftop of the Cine Society, with the city as a backdrop, settle back comfortably into a deckchair with a cocktail in hand as you prepare to (re)discover a classic film under the stars.

> **Cinemateca**

The Cinemateca has the best film programme in Portugal, hands down. And, in summer, it also screens quality films on a delightfully secluded terrace, taking you on a real trip back in time, far from the tourist crowds. Before the screening, you can also dine alfresco and visit the Cinemateca bookshop, a paradise for film buffs.

Open-air films generally start at around 9.30pm. As a general rule, you must purchase tickets on site and cannot reserve them in advance – with one exception: if you book a table for dinner on the terrace just before an evening screening, you can also reserve tickets for the film.

CINE SOCIETY
CARMO ROOFTOP
TERRAÇOS DO CARMO

Instagram: @cinesociety.lisbon
cinesociety.pt

CINEMATECA
RUA BARATA SALGUEIRO 39

Programme: cinemateca.pt/Programacao.aspx
Tickets can be reserved by booking a table for dinner: contact the restaurant 39 Degraus
+351 960 396 370 or + 351 911 904 075

#05

THREE BAR STOOLS, **ONE BAR**

It's a Portuguese spirit(s)ual question, but there is a world beyond port wine. And, in this world, Ginja, or Ginjinha (sour-cherry liqueur), holds centre stage. For a long time, the Ginjinha Sem Rival (Unrivalled Ginjinha) bar, which opened in 1890, made its own in the back shop. And the question customers are asked the moment they rest their elbows on the counter hasn't changed since the 19th century: 'Com o sem elas?' (With or without cherries?) We recommend with – even though (or especially because) it's dangerous! Your little glass will be served filled to the brim, as tradition dictates. As for whether or not it's truly the best Ginjinha, you'll simply have to head across the street to try out the neighbouring bar's version for yourself ...

GINJINHA SEM RIVAL
R. PORTAS DE SANTO ANTÃO 7

+351 21 346 8231

GINJINHA SEM RIVAL
DE
J. Manuel L. Cima
EDUARDINO (EXCLUSIVO)
· MARCA REGISTADA ·
GINJA SEM RIVAL

#06

ROOMS WITH VIEWS: **LISBON AT YOUR FEET**

Put your heart-to-heart with Lisbon on hold for the night? No, thanks. Instead, choose to fall asleep with Lisbon at the foot of your bed and wake up to the same vision, daytime version. Here is a selection of rooms we recommend:

> **Memmo Alfama**

This hotel is hidden away in the Alfama district, at the end of a cul-de-sac paved with uneven cobblestones. Up on the roof terrace, slide into the red swimming pool to do a few laps with a view. And in rooms 31 and 33, the Alfama is right there at the foot of the bed, a labyrinth of rooftops unfurling all the way down to the Mar da Palha (Sea of Straw).

€€€

MEMMO ALFAMA
TV. MERCEEIRAS 27

+351 21 049 5660

memmohotels.com/alfama
Instagram: @memmoalfama

Torel Palace

© CARLOS VIEIRA

> **Torel Palace Lisbon**

A great location at the top of the Hill of Sant'Ana, just a few steps from the Jardim do Torel. Regardless of what room you're staying in, the terrace, swimming pool and royal peace and quiet await you. But we recommend putting your bags down in room 6, 8 or 28: big windows, small balcony and an insane view of the heart of the city.

€€€

TOREL PALACE LISBON
R. CÂMARA PESTANA 45

+351 21 829 0810

torelpalacelisbon.com
Instagram: @torelpalace_lisbon

MEMMO ALFAMA

#07

RUNNING LAPS **ON A ROOFTOP**

Enter the hotel, walk confidently towards the elevator, get in and push the '-1' button. When you reach the spa, buy a day pass. Get changed and take the elevator to the 11th floor. A vision overlooking the Tagus: a running track on the roof. So you can race against the sun and challenge the clouds, legs in the air, eyes taking in a 360°-view of Lisbon. Pure magic.*

*Since this magic is on the pricey side, this 5-star running experience is a good gift idea. A day pass includes admission to the fitness room and spa. We guarantee that you (or the recipient of your gift) won't regret it.

€€€

FOUR SEASONS HOTEL RITZ LISBON
R. RODRIGO DA FONSECA 88

+351 21 381 1400

fourseasons.com

#08

GO FOR A STROLL **IN THE ESTUFA FRIA**

The greenhouse in the north of Eduardo VII Park is reminiscent of a Rousseau painting. Huge plants tickle the sky. Well, almost – this is a greenhouse, after all, so wooden blinds form a roof overhead ... even as they let the sunlight filter in. Come late in the afternoon, when the day is gently fading and the sky turning pink. To the left of the central alley, a small door leads to the arid and tropical greenhouse (Estufa Fria). Giant banana plants, cactuses that defy all norms ... Where in the world are we? Right in the heart of the city!

ESTUFA FRIA
PARQUE EDUARDO VII

+351 21 817 0996

estufafria.lisboa.pt

© THOMAS JONGLEZ

09

AN AMERICAN DINER, **LUSITANIAN STYLE**

Galeto, a Lisbon institution founded in 1966, is the perfect place to have lunch or dinner near the Gulbenkian Museum, just a few minutes walk away. And if you're hungry during the night, it closes at 3:30am ...

The venue takes up a concept imported from Brazil – a succession of counters where you sit side by side on stools fixed to the floor, like an American diner, Lusitanian style.

The menu lines up the great classics of Portuguese cuisine, but people tend to go there for its ambience and concept rather than its gastronomy.

A classic, not yet discovered by tourists.

GALETO
AVENIDA DA REPÚBLICA 14

Daily 7:30am / 3:30am

+351 21 354 4444

© LUCIE ETCHEBERS

Vinhos
Espirituosas
Cervejas
KETCHUP
CLÁSSICO

A VIDA PORTUGUESA
LARGO DO INTENDENTE PINA MANIQUE 23

+351 21 197 4512

avidaportuguesa.com
Instagram: @avidaportuguesa

#10

LISBON'S BEST **CONCEPT STORE**

This is the Portuguese answer to Eataly – but not just for edibles. This concept store, the biggest of the four spaces created on the initiative of Catarina Portas, brings together the best artisanal products from all over Portugal. Its 500 square metres progress through an evolution from one room to the next. First, there's the living room, where the wool blankets will make you want to settle down for a nap; then you take a turn towards the kitchen, between ceramics and gourmet food products, before finally ogling the stationery items and ointments. Everything has been carefully selected and is beautifully presented. We double dare you to leave empty-handed.

A VIDA PORTUGUESA
© LOLA INTENDENTE

#11

DIVE INTO **LISBON'S SECRET UNDERGROUND**

It's easy to pass Desterro without noticing: no inscription, no sign to be seen on this anonymous door along the Calçada of that name (not to be confused with Rua or Travessa do Desterro ...).

Only locals know about this secret nocturnal refuge away from the tourist trail – 'desterro' is Portuguese for 'exile'.

A small bar on the ground floor, dance floor in the basement. In an intimate atmosphere reminiscent of Berlin's heyday, you can listen to quality electro or techno.

Just a hint to help you find the place, because it's worth the effort: not far from the Cervejaria Ramiro restaurant on Avenida Almirante Reis, look out for Calçada do Desterro, then knock at the right door ...

CLUB DESTERRO
CALÇADA DO DESTERRO

€

Wednesday-Saturday, 10pm / 4am

Membership card at entrance: €3

#12

AN APERITIF UNDER THE STARS ON LISBON STEPS

When you've had enough of cod, head to this little restaurant in an alleyway of the old Mouraria district. Opened in 2012, this is the city's first fully vegan restaurant. In this unique venue you can simultaneously meet regulars, local residents and passing travellers seated directly on the steps transformed into terraces. On sunny days, musicians play at the foot of the steps, as in an open-air amphitheatre – perfect for a drink at the end of the day. The menu, creative and seasonal, changes regularly. Remember to book, especially in summer.

THE FOOD TEMPLE
BECO DO JASMIM 18

+351 21 887 4397

thefoodtemple.com
Instagram: @the_food_temple

THE FOOD TEMPLE © TAMARA SEILMAN

© LUCILE [illegible]

THE FOOD TEMPLE © MARIA MEDICI

13

SMALL CAFE, **WIDE ANGLE**

Exploring, walking, climbing, running ... That's all well and good, but where's the R&R in all this? It's right here, at this cafe under a theatre. Take a little break and settle down in one of the armchairs facing the enormous windows – just long enough to bring your heart rate back down, check in with yourself and drink a latte while taking in the panoramic view of Lisbon.

€

CAFÉ DA GARAGEM
TEATRO TABORDA
COSTA DO CASTELO 75

+351 21 885 4190

Instagram: @cafe.dagaragem
teatrodagaragem.com/en/cafe-da-garagem

CAFÉ DA GARAGEM

#14

UNCOVER THE SECRET **SPOT WHERE FADO SINGERS HIDE AWAY**

First, you find yourself facing a heavy blue wooden door adorned with a gilded handle: magisterial, intimidating. Then you attempt to open it before realising that you have to ring the bell. Someone opens the door for you. It's here, in the dim interior of this 18th-century building decorated with old azulejo tiles, that the city's fado singers meet up after having sung their hearts out elsewhere.

The musicians gradually trickle into their sanctuary. Around 11pm, a fadista sings the saudade accompanied by two guitar players, linking gesture with voice, emotion with the expression in their eyes ... A few minutes later, another voice, other musicians, will take over, but the thrill remains the same: fado. And the performance doesn't let up until sleep finally wins out – sometimes at 2am, sometimes not until breakfast.

MESA DE FRADES
R. DOS REMÉDIOS 139

+351 91 702 9436	mesadefrades.pt	Instagram: @mesadefrades

Restaurante / Restaurant
Mesa
de Frades

#15

A FANTASTIC BAR **THAT HAS RESISTED ALFAMA'S GENTRIFICATION**

Among the few places in Alfama that have resisted gentrification, the Tejo Bar is a wonderfully intimate venue where you come across an audience of connoisseurs who know how to appreciate places that have kept their soul. Listen to quality music in a warm and truly local atmosphere, where some regulars even serve themselves at the bar ...

And if you're in the mood and can sing, play piano or guitar, feel free to launch a jam session.

Magic happens here, night after night. And they do an excellent Caipirinha.

TEJO BAR
BECO DO VIGÁRIO 1A,
ALFAMA

€

+351 966 388 870	Instagram: @tejobar.oficial	Entry: €5

#16

COLOURFUL CUISINE

Turning into a narrow alley in Alfama, you'll find Roda Viva, the best Mozambican restaurant in Lisbon. The owner, Chamba, a former *pizzaiolo*, is both friendly and professional. He's been a chef since 2014, using recipes mainly inherited from his grandmother: a clever mix of flavours from Africa, India and Macau. For example, you can gorge on crab and shrimp curries, a delicious chicken with peanuts and some emblematic homely dishes such as *mathapa* (cassava leaf and coconut sauce), Chamba's favourite dish. His secret to success? 'Being happy and in a good mood', undoubtedly the best recipe handed down by his dear grandmother. Don't leave without a pot of homemade spicy sauce.

€

RODA VIVA
BECO DO MEXIAS, 11

+351 21 887 1730

roda-viva.eatbu.com
Instagram: @rodavivarestaurante

VAGO
© LUIS GALA

LISA
© @SHOTBYTEJA

#17

MUSIC, COCKTAILS **AND TAPAS**

Opened in late 2021 by globetrotting DJs of Colombian, Brazilian, Turkish and Portuguese heritage, Vago is just what Lisbon's nightlife scene was missing. In the early evening, head here to listen to a fantastic music programme (house, techno, samba, zouk, afrobeat ...), have a drink (great cocktails) and eat delicious *petiscos* (Portuguese-style tapas) created by chef Leonor Godinho. Later in the night, come to dance – and more.

Run by the same owners, Lisa is just a few buildings further down on the same street. Every night, it features live DJs and musicians playing jazz, contemporary music, rock, folk, electro and more.

VAGO **RUA DAS GAIVOTAS 11A**	**LISA** **RUA DAS GAIVOTAS 5**
Instagram: @vago.lisboa	salalisa.pt Instagram: @a.sala.lisa

€

GABINETE
LISBON BREAKFAST

#18

A UNIQUE **TEA EMPORIUM**

Located in a magnificent former 19th-century shoe shop, the Companhia Portugueza do Chá (Portuguese Tea Company) is a small gem: the moment you open the door, you're enveloped by the powerful scent of this leaf, which, according to the 5th- or 6th-century Chinese Buddhist monk Bodhidharma, promotes concentration and meditation.

Ensconced on lacquered shelves, the elegant tins hold 250 blends of tea: varieties from the most prized plantations in India, Nepal, Sri Lanka (Ceylon), China, Japan, Taiwan, Vietnam and Korea, as well as from Latin America, Africa and the Azores ...

The blends, flavoured with organic fruit or flowers, are created by the Argentinian owner, Sebastian Filgueiras. In his workshop at the back, Sebastian also regularly dreams up new flavours: Japanese yuzu and green tea, black tea with grapefruit, and fruit infusions that are perfect for enjoying iced.

€

COMPANHIA PORTUGUEZA DO CHÁ
R. DO POÇO DOS NEGROS 105

+351 21 395 1614

companhiaportuguezadocha.com

雪山

كوسومار
COSUMAR

PORTUGUEZA
COMPANHIA
VIEIRA &

- SEBASTIAN FILGUEIRAS -

FOUNDER OF COMPANHIA PORTUGUEZA DO CHÁ

Where did you get the idea for this tea emporium?

In Lisbon, small shops that combined the coffee and tea trades had become obsolete, and I wanted to revive this tradition by expanding the range of varieties available and constantly raising the quality. Catherine of Braganza (1638–1705), who made tea fashionable in Europe, has pride of place here: it's her profile that is featured on our tea tins. In the 18th century, every garden in the city had tea pavilions, a legacy of the strong ties between Portugal and the East.

What's your favourite tea?

The loose-leaf tea of my childhood – usually black tea from China, Assam or

Ceylon. Strong teas. In northern Portugal, where my wife grew up, serving black tea to children before school – and in hospital too – was also very common. Very often it was tea from Mozambique or Ceylon. Tea bags didn't come along until much later.

What inspires your blends?

The light of this city, the culture of this country, its literature, its history ... I started with Lisbon Breakfast, a blend of Ceylon tea and black tea grown in the Azores. It's bright and well-balanced, a good everyday morning tea. Our Earl Grey Portugal is flavoured with the peel of bergamot grown on a farm in the Alentejo region: we dry it ourselves. Many of our teas are exclusive.

What's the rarest tea available here?

Thousand-Year Tea. It's grown in the Yunnan region of China, and what makes it unique is that its leaves are picked from a single tree, probably one of the oldest in the world. It's even listed as one of China's heritage tea trees. The taste is impossible to define – it's mild yet powerful. I put myself on a waiting list for this tea every year ... and never receive more than 2 kg.

#19

BAR, BOOKSTORE, CINEMA, CONCERTS, DJ SETS ... **AN ESSENTIAL VENUE**

It was the cultural venue that was missing in Lisbon and a long-time dream of owner José Pinho, founder of bookstore Ler Devagar in the LX Factory west of central Lisbon.

In the middle of Bairro Alto, this former outbuilding of a three-storey convent is a refuge for locals. They gather here at the end of their busy days to have a drink, a bite to eat or simply take a break.

The building also has a bookstore, film screenings, exhibitions, live concerts and DJ sets.

In a very relaxed atmosphere, the bar serves some mouthwatering snacks including a 'pulled pork' mushroom sandwich to die for and much else. All this can be enjoyed in the Museu da Preguiça (Museum of Laziness), a room with beds. A rest before finally joining the dance floor.

CASA DO COMUM
RUA DA ROSA 285
BAIRRO ALTO

€

casadocomum.org

Instragram: @casadocomum

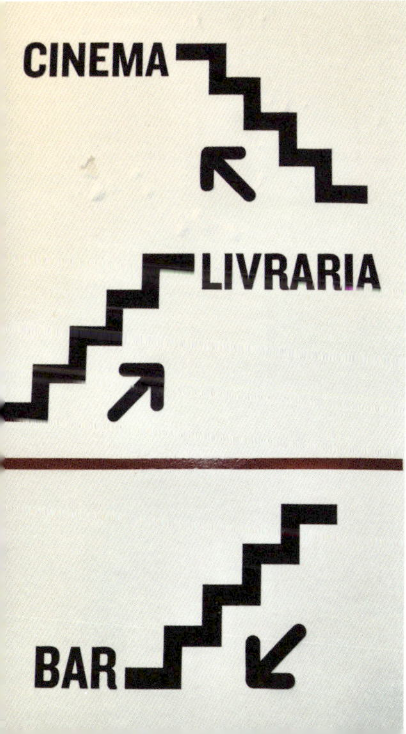
CINEMA
LIVRARIA
BAR

#20

A HISTORIC VENUE, FAR FROM THE IN-CROWDS OF TOURISTS

SNOB, not far from Príncipe Real, is a historic venue that has kept the old-fashioned charm of its early days in the 1960s. We love the hushed and confidential atmosphere, the chic and timeless decor, the cocktails, the attentive and thoughtful service, and the fact that you have to ring the doorbell to get in ...

If some people simply come for a drink, others come to savour the famous bife à Snob (steak with an egg on top), a house special that's been on the menu for five decades.

The bar-restaurant provided a secret refuge for politicians, journalists, revolutionaries and intellectuals during the dictatorship. Among the regulars was writer José Saramago. SNOB was taken over in 1975 by Albino Oliveira, shortly after the 'Carnation Revolution'.

BAR-RESTAURANT SNOB
RUA DE O SÉCULO 178

+351 926 459 164

snobbar.pt
reservas@snobbar.pt

Instagram: @snobbar.pt

TOQUE À
CAMPAINHA
RING THE BELL

#21

SOAK UP THE ATMOSPHERE OF PRAÇA DAS FLORES

In Lisbon, all roads lead to the charming Praça das Flores, a small shady square in the heart of the Príncipe Real district. Its fountain, lavender-blue kiosk and wooden benches make it look like a cinema decor. However, what draws visitors there most often are the multitude of bars, restaurants and shops scattered about the area. During the day the atmosphere is peaceful. You can daydream with a coffee accompanied by the famous Portuguese egg custard tart known as *pastel de nata*. However, as soon as the sun goes down, 'Flower Square' comes alive. People meet there to have a drink, something to eat or just enjoy the sweet evenings in Lisbon.

In the square itself, at **Magnolia**, you sit on the terrace (or at the only indoor table near the open window overlooking the square) to share some tapas and a good glass of wine. The signature dish of the restaurant: oven-cooked Camembert sprinkled with honey.

€€

MAGNOLIA
PRAÇA DAS FLORES 43

+351 93 531 5373

Instagram: @magnolia_lisboa

© LUCIE ETCHEBERS

Close to the square, **Marquise da Møbler** is the most charming tea room / concept store in Príncipe Real. All the objects you'll see around are for sale. Its little secret is the interior patio hidden from the street. Perfect for breakfast or brunch.

In front of the kiosk, the **Black Sheep** offers one of the best selections of wines in Lisbon. From time to time the owner and chief wine waiter Lucas Ferreira takes out his guitar to accompany the tranquility that reigns on the square.

€

MARQUISE DA MØBLER
RUA NOVA DA PIEDADE 33

+351 96 661 1192
Instagram: @marquisedamobler

€€

BLACK SHEEP
PRAÇA DAS FLORES 62

+351 93 894 6762
blacksheeplisboa.com
Instagram: @blacksheeplisboa

MARQUISE DA MØBLER

FOXTROT
28
Alarme
FOX
TROT

#22

JUST OUR KIND
OF BAR

Behind its Art Nouveau façade, Foxtrot is a historic bar established by Luís Pinto Coelho (who's also behind the magnificent but over-touristic Pavilhão Chinês bar).

We love its welcoming vibe, crystal globe-lamps, cosy boudoirs and velvety benches, evoking the snug atmosphere of an old English pub.

Between two (good) cocktails, you can also play pool or order food, notably the prego no pão (meat sandwich), a Lisbon classic.

FOXTROT BAR
TV. DE SANTA TERESA 28

+351 213 952 697 | barfoxtrot.pt | Instagram: @barfoxtrot

© THOMAS JONGLEZ

© LUCIE ETCHEBERS

© FOX TROT

© FOX TROT

#23

A BAR
OFF THE BEATEN TRACK

Since 1972, the little red door to this nightclub has seen many insiders pass through, here to lose all sense of time. In fact, in the small room, where waiters flit about in bow ties, styles and centuries seem to collapse in on themselves: tasselled lampshades brush against armchairs, knick-knacks flirt with illustrations from the 1930s ... To make sure you don't miss a thing, choose the table at the back perched on a small platform or a seat at the bar, while sipping a Caipï or Amendoa Amarga.

NB: Since we're still sort of stuck in 1972 here, smoking is permitted.

PROCÓPIO
ALTO DE SÃO FRANCISCO 21

+351 21 385 2851

barprocopio.com/pt

#24

PASTÉIS DE NATA VS ELEPHANT EARS: **SHOWDOWN OF THE SWEETS**

PASTÉIS DE NATA

If Lisbon had a flavour, it would be the *pastel de nata* (custard tart) – never mind that this pastry was actually invented in the 19th century by nuns in the convent in Belém (which was still separate from Lisbon at the time). Since 1837, the Pastelaria de Belém has been carrying on this tradition, selling these *pastel de Belém* pastries to the hordes of tourists who come here to taste the original – the one that started it all. But you can also avoid a long wait: at the Aloma pastry shop and tea salon, which has won the prize for best *pastel de nata* more than once, the custard tarts are prepared on the spot, served lukewarm, dusted with cinnamon ... and polished off at the counter in less time than it took to write this sentence. For the most patient among you, treat yourself to the pastel de nata at the superb Jardim da Estrela, located close by.

PASTELARIA ALOMA
R. FRANCISCO METRASS 67

Instagram: @pastelaria_aloma
aloma.pt

PASTELARIA O CARECA
R. DUARTE PACHECO PEREIRA 11D

+351 21 301 0987
pastelariaocareca.pt
Instagram: @pastelariacareca

ELEPHANT EARS

Above Belém, in the Restelo neighbourhood, the Pastelaria O Careca is a local institution. Regulars throng to what they call 'the Bald Guy' – the nickname given to the man who originally opened the place in 1954. The price of success? You now have to take a number at the door and wait a few minutes for your turn – just long enough to peruse the amazing display case before choosing the house speciality: elephant-ear cookies. But not just any old elephant ears, the best in town: the perfect balance of flaky, toasted, lightly caramelized, crunchy and sweet.

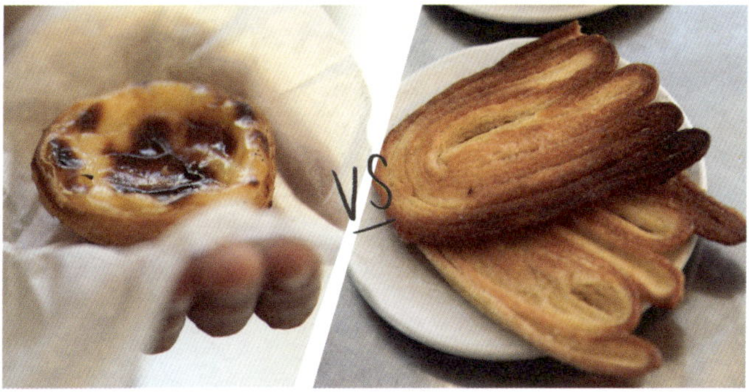

#25

A BISTRO JUST **THE WAY WE LIKE IT**

A little way from the touristy areas (which is a relief!), in the pleasant Campo de Ourique district, yet barely a 15-minutes' walk from Principe Real, Bichomau is our kind of bistro: 100% Lisbon, with its pretty blue ceramic decor, excellent food (a new take on Portuguese cuisine) at reasonable prices and a charming atmosphere ... What more could you want?

One of our favourite places in Lisbon.

BISTRÔ BICHOMAU
R. COELHO DA ROCHA 21A

+351 21 160 8694

reservation.umai.io/en/widget/bistro-bicho-mau

BRANCOS

WINE BOTTLES

#26

A MASTERPIECE **OF A JAPANESE RESTAURANT**

With only ten seats around a 'U' counter, Omakase Ri is an exceptional Japanese restaurant where you feel almost privileged to have found a place.

No menu is available (you just tell the very friendly team serving you of any food intolerances). After that, for the next two hours (which pass quickly) you're treated to a parade of dishes whose finesse, refinement and precision are spectacular. As Japanese tradition demands, everything is also beautifully presented and the products used are the freshest they could be. For example, wasabi comes not in a tube but fresh, as in the best restaurants in Japan. Not to be missed.

OMAKASE RI
RUA GARCIA DE ORTA 71C
SHOPPING LAPA 71 STORE 1

+351 91 409 4506
omakaseri.com
Instagram: @omakase.ri

Strongly advised to book well in advance or count on a bit of luck for last-minute places

RESTAURANTE PONTO FINAL

PONTO FINAL
CAIS DO GINJAL 72
CACILHAS
ALMADA

€€

+351 93 686 9031

Instagram: @pontofinalrest

#27

GRILLED FISH **AT PONTO FINAL**

A short boat ride and 15 minutes later you're in Cacilhas, on the other side of the Tagus. Grab the table at the very end of the pier, directly across from Lisbon. Murmuring water, the light of the final hours of the day, the simplicity of grilled fish with just a twist of lemon ... If this isn't happiness, it sure comes close.

RESTAURANTE
PONTO
FINAL

PONTO FINAL

#28

EXPERIENCE
A SURREAL EVENING

About 15 minutes east of central Lisbon by taxi, in the Beato district, the Palacio do Grilo (Palace of the Cricket), which was classified as a monument of public interest in 2011, is a magnificent 18th-century palace. A few years ago, it was transformed into a spectacular restaurant-cum-nightclub with a deliberately surreal atmosphere.

During dinner, which is served in the palace's magnificent main rooms, expect improbable artistic performances amidst the tables. The food is decent – but that's not why you're here.

After dinner, at weekends, head for the nightclub, where the DJs and bar staff, donning costumes and sometimes masks, set the tone for a decidedly offbeat evening.

One-of-a kind in Lisbon

PALACIO DO GRILO

PALACIO DO GRILO – GALA CRICRI
CALÇADA DO DUQUE DE LAFÕES 1

+351 91 044 0942

palaciogrilo.com
galacricri.com

Instagram: @palaciodogrilo and @galacricri

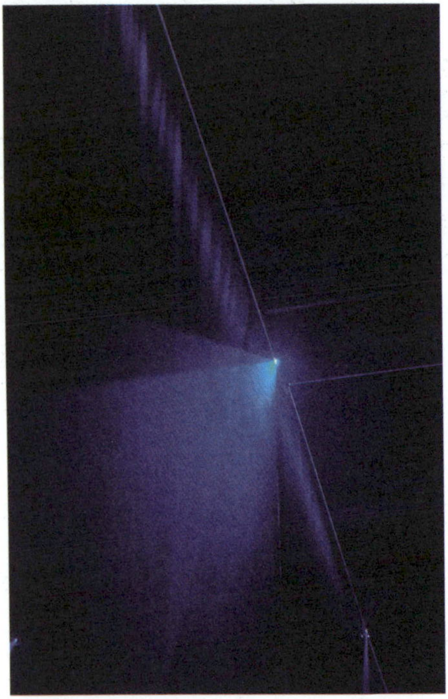

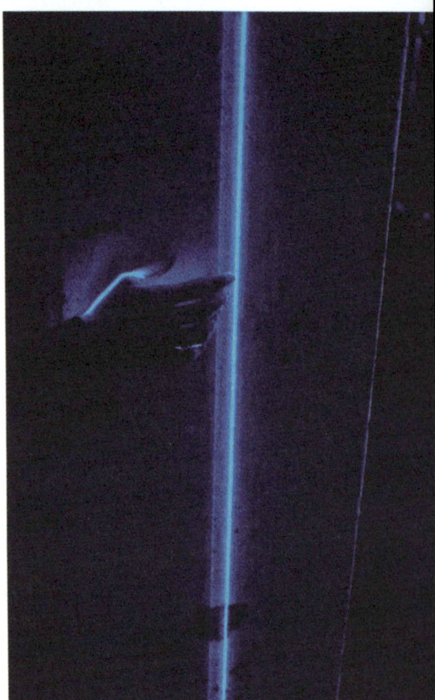

#29

A BERLIN CLUB
IN LISBON

Rumours spread across the city like wildfire in 2023 when Outra Cena opened in a disused former winery in Marvila. Success was immediate, maybe because there was no other place like it in Lisbon, and there still isn't.

In this huge concrete cathedral, the atmosphere is industrial and, as in the founding nightclub in Berlin (Berghain), phones are banned. This lets you stop filming and taking photos, instead giving you the rare opportunity to live in the moment, to let go completely and dance like there's no tomorrow. And it feels good ..

The club frequently attracts big names from the electronic scene.

€

OUTRA CENA
AVENIDA INFANTE DOM HENRIQUE 0

Instragram: @outracena_lisboa

Playlist: tinyurl.com/3upx474z

#30

DISCOVERING **THE EAST OF THE CITY**

In Marvila, to the east of the city, a neighbourhood that's constantly moving up and up, 8 Marvila is a sprawling 22,000-square-metre warehouse conversion. It was originally built in 1917 to store as much as 5 million litres of Pereira da Fonseca wine in vast vats that now house the new venues.

The cultural and commercial space offers everything from an eclectic interior design store to vegetarian doughnuts, Mexican and Japanese restaurants alongside vintage clothes, vinyl records, a pizzeria, an upscale garden centre called Planta Livre, astrology, reiki and massage therapies. There's also eight paddle tennis courts and even an indoor Pickleball court.

8 MARVILA
PRAÇA DAVID LEANDRO DA SILVA 8

8marvila.com

Instagram: @8marvila

TATTOO

ABEL PEREIRA DA FONSECA
ABEL PEREIRA DA FONSECA

Go check it out quickly as the privately owned space is destined for a mega luxury real-estate project.

Don't miss the Night Market until midnight on Saturdays, or the organic brunches at Dear Breakfast alongside restaurant and bar MATO's vegetarian pizzas.

The Outra Cena club (see p. 123) is literally glued to 8 Marvila and the wonderful Fábrica Braço de Prata (Silver Arms Factory, p. 131) is a 3-minute walk away ...

© RUPERTEDEN

SAÍDA

#31

AN ALTERNATIVE NIGHT OUT
IN MARVILA

Nights out in the east of Lisbon, between Marvila's industrial relics and the cultural revival, have never been so lively.

Housed in a long-abandoned former ammunitions factory, hence its name ('Silver Arms Factory'), the Fábrica Braço de Prata has been the city's most interesting alternative location since 2007.

This immense space (twelve rooms) where restaurant, concerts, exhibitions, literary meetings, plays, dance classes and raves are interwoven, is constantly reinventing itself. Explore and be inspired.

FÁBRICA BRAÇO DE PRATA
RUA DA FÁBRICA DO MATERIAL DE GUERRA 1
MARVILA

€

fabricabracodeprata.com	Instagram: @fabricabracodeprata

Limonada caseira 2,5
Cerveja (Dois Corvos)

In this collection, the final address won't always be revealed to you, as it's too confidential. Up to you to find it!

#32

THE SECRET CHINESE RESTAURANT
YOU NEEDED, OF COURSE

In Mouraria district, look for the blue door in Rua Marquês Ponte de Lima.
Press the red button on the intercom.
Show your credentials and go up a floor.
Order the dumplings.
You're welcome.

SECRET ADDRESS

34

MUITO OBRIGADO / MANY THANKS TO

Jérôme C, João-Maria MS, Sofia M, Peter O, Chloé S, Miguel C, Miguel J, Alexander W, Nelson P, Rita A, Luca P, Ruben O and Anne-Laure B

This book was created by:
Fany Péchiodat, Lauriane Gepner and Lucie Etchebers, authors
Coline Girard, illustrator
Paula Franco @lisbonbylight, photographer (unless otherwise stated)
Emmanuelle Willard Toulemonde, layout
Sophie Schlondorff and Sonny Alexander, translation
Jana Gough and Caroline Lawrence, editing
Kimberly Bess, proofreading
Mado de La Quintinie, publishing

Cover photo: © Adobe Stock / Stockbym

You can write to us at info@editionsjonglez.com
Follow us on Instagram: @jonglez_publishing

From the same publisher

Photo Books

Abandoned America: The age of Consequences
Abandoned Asylums
Abandoned Australia
Abandoned Belgium
Abandoned Churches: Unclaimed Places of Worship
Abandoned Cinemas of the World
Abandoned France
Abandoned Germany
Abandoned Lebanon
Abandoned Italy
Abandoned Japan
Abandoned Spain
Abandoned USSR
Abandoned World – An AI-generated exploration
After the Final Curtain: The Fall of the American Movie Theater
After the Final Curtain: America's Abandoned Theaters
Baikonur – Vestiges of the Soviet Space Program
Cinemas – A French Heritage
Chernobyl's Atomic Legacy – 25 years after disaster
Clickbait – A visual journey through AI-generated stories
Destination: Wellness – Our 35 best places in the world to take time out
Forbidden Places – Exploring our Abandoned Heritage
Forgotten Heritage
Oblivion
Parisian Theatres – Exceptional Venues
Secret Art Nouveau
Secret Sacred Sites
The cinemas of India – An exceptional heritage
Venice deserted
Venice from the skies

'Confidential' and 'Soul of' Guides

Berlin Confidential
Los Angeles Confidential
Malta Confidential
Marrakesh Confidential
Munich Confidential
New York City Confidential
Paris Confidential

Soul of Amsterdam - A guide to the 30 best experiences
Soul of Athens – 30 experiences
Soul of Barcelona – 30 experiences
Soul of Brussels – A guide to exceptional experiences
Soul of Detroit – A guide to exceptional experiences
Soul of Kyoto – A guide to exceptional experiences
Soul of Marseille – A guide to exceptional experiences
Soul of Milan – A guide to exceptional experiences
Soul of Rome – A guide to exceptional experiences
Soul of Tokyo – A guide to exceptional experiences
Soul of Venice – A guide to exceptional experiences
Soul of Vienna – A guide to exceptional experiences

Registration of copyright: September 2026 – Edition: 01
ISBN: 978-2-38715-081-3
Printed in June 2026 in Bulgaria by Dedrax